SLAVE SHIP CAPTAIN

John Newton (1725–1807) went to sea and
became a ship's captain – but his ship was a slave
trading ship. His heart was touched by the misery
he saw around him. From London he worked
hard to kill the slave trade which had once given
him his livelihood.

STORIES OF FAITH AND FAME

BISHOP JIM
Joyce Reason — The Story of James Hannington

CONQUEROR OF DARKNESS
Phyllis Garlick — The Story of Helen Keller

CRUSADER FOR CHRIST
Jean Wilson — The Story of Billy Graham

EVER OPEN DOOR
C. Scott — The Story of Dr Barnardo

FRIEND OF THE CHIEFS
Iris Clinton — The Story of Robert Moffat

FROM SLAVE BOY TO BISHOP
John Milsome — The Story of Samuel Adjai Crowther

GOD'S ARCTIC ADVENTURER
Constance Savery — The Story of William Bompas

GOD'S MADCAP
Nancy E. Robbins — The Story of Amy Carmichael

GOLDEN FOOT
J. R. Batten — The Story of Judson of Burma

HORSEMAN OF THE KING
Cyril Davey — The Story of John Wesley

LADY WITH A LAMP
Cyril Davey — The Story of Florence Nightingale

MILLIONAIRE FOR GOD
J. Erskine — The Story of C. T. Studd

NEVER SAY DIE
Cyril Davey — The Story of Gladys Aylward

NIGHT OF THE SNOWS
R. G. Martin — The Story of Wilfred Grenfell

ON THE CLOUDS TO CHINA
Cyril Davey — The Story of Hudson Taylor

PROPHET OF THE PACIFIC
Margaret Kabell — The Story of John G. Paton

QUAKER CAVALIER
Joyce Reason — The Story of William Penn

SAINT IN THE SLUMS
Cyril Davey — The Story of Kagawa of Japan

SEARCHER FOR GOD
Joyce Reason — The Story of Isobel Kuhn

SLAVE SHIP CAPTAIN
Carolyn Scott — The Story of John Newton

SOUTH SEAS SAILOR
Cecil Northcott — The Story of John Williams

STAR OVER GOBI
Cecil Northcott — The Story of Mildred Cable

THE DOCTOR WHO NEVER GAVE UP
C. Scott — The Story of Dr Ida Scudder

THE HEROINE OF NEWGATE
John Milsome — The Story of Elizabeth Fry

THE MAN WHO FREED SLAVES
Elsie M. Johnson — The Story of William Wilberforce

THE MONK WHO SHOOK THE WORLD
Cyril Davey — The Story of Martin Luther

TO BE A PILGRIM
Joyce Reason — The Story of John Bunyan

TRAIL MAKER
R. V. Latham — The Story of David Livingstone

WHITE QUEEN
Donald McFarlan — The Story of Mary Slessor

WIZARD OF THE GREAT LAKE
Donald McFarlan — The Story of Alexander Mackay

YOUNG MAN IN A HURRY
Iris Clinton — The Story of William Carey

SLAVE SHIP CAPTAIN

The Story of John Newton

by
CAROLYN SCOTT

LUTTERWORTH PRESS
CAMBRIDGE

Lutterworth Press
P.O. Box 60
Cambridge CB1 2NT

British Library Cataloguing in Publication Data available

ISBN 0 7188 2245 5

Copyright © 1971 Carolyn Scott

First published 1971 by Lutterworth Press
First paperback edition 1975
Reprinted 1982, 1988

Cover illustration by Elissa Vial

Printed and bound in Great Britain by
Cox & Wyman Ltd, Reading

CONTENTS

		page
1	PRESS-GANG VICTIM	7
2	DESERTING THE SHIP	13
3	"I WANT TO MAKE MY FORTUNE"	21
4	ON THE SLAVE COAST	32
5	FEVER-STRICKEN ISLAND	39
6	SMUGGLING THE LETTER	50
7	THE VOICE IN THE STORM	55
8	FIRST MATE ON THE SLAVER	65
9	IN COMMAND OF THE SHIP	75
10	PREACHER AND PROPHET	83
11	THE END OF SLAVE TRADING	88

1

PRESS-GANG VICTIM

WINTER was nearly over. John was fourteen years old. One night, he left his father's home in Rotherhithe to walk by the river. He wanted to be alone.

Mists swirled up from the water. He glanced curiously down the creeks by the wharves. He had heard that convicts escaped that way in the dead of night, only to be caught again by the coast-guards on duty day and night along the river.

Fog mingled with the mist, and John shivered. His footsteps echoed on the wet boards. He turned his collar up and hugged the thin cotton round him. He wished he was wearing a thick coat on top of his light checked sailor shirt.

The noise of shouting and singing drew him to a tavern built on the dockside, and as he stepped into the doorway, the bright light of the oil lamps made him blink. Ordering a short draught of rum, he drank it slowly, leaning against the wall, watching people as they came and went, the damp steaming out of their clothes in the fuggy warmth.

John finished his drink and made his way out again, into the mist. It was raining quite fast by now. To shorten the journey home, he cut across the docks. He hadn't gone far before he heard footsteps following him. He quickened his pace, and the footsteps hurried too.

"You, lad!" The voice was harsh, and it had a note of command in it. John turned. He was facing a tall man, dressed in the clothes of a naval officer. John seemed to remember his face.

"Which ship are you from?" The man's eyes were on John's shirt.

Then John remembered. It was just now, in the tavern. But the man hadn't been alone then. He had been talking with three friends, and John had noticed how they kept glancing at people as they came in, watching all the time, as if they were looking for someone. And now he had the cheek to speak as if he was speaking to the lowest man on board.

John hesitated, searching for a suitably haughty reply. As he hesitated he realized, too late, that the man wasn't alone, and that his clothes were not the clothes of a merchant seaman—they were the clothes of a lieutenant in the king's navy.

John turned to run. Before he had gone two steps, he felt a blow on his shoulder, and then another on his head.

"Don't struggle, and you won't get hurt," grunted the man gruffly. As he fell, they were on top of him, pinning his arms behind his back. He kicked and shouted as they half dragged, half carried him to a small boat waiting, silent and unnoticed, hidden in the black shadow of the wharf. His feet stumbled under him as they pushed him up over the side and on to the boat. Then he was thrown head first through the hatchway into the pitch-black hold.

Before he could recover himself, John heard the grating of heavy bolts being made fast above the hatch. Then there was silence. He had been press-ganged into service on a man-of-war.

It was a long time before he could see anything in the darkness. Gradually he began to make out shapes and movement. Then, as his ears grew accustomed to the sound of the boat and the sea, he began to hear other noises.

He wasn't alone. There were more people imprisoned in the semi-darkness, coughing and grumbling and trying to sleep in the slimy dampness of the hold of the little boat *Betsey*, as it bobbed up and down by the wharf-side.

John wasn't going to give in as easily as they had.

He shouted and screamed at the hatchway, battering the door until his knuckles bled. No one took any notice. The men in the hold with him had seen it all before. They knew it was no use. And outside, they were far away in the dockland, searching for more men to complete the number of recruits required by HMS *Harwich*, at anchor in the Thames estuary, before she could begin convoy duty, guarding the British coasts from French invaders.

It was 1739. John's father was a sea captain, and already John could handle a ship as well as any man. He had been at sea since he was nine years old. He had spent a year working in Spain—he would have been there still if he hadn't hated it so much that he had worked his passage home.

But he didn't feel wanted at home. Long ago he remembered his mother saying, "If you do what is right, God will love you and look after you." But his mother was dead. And since his father married again, John felt that no one wanted him, let alone God. Except that he had decided there was no God.

Fourteen wasn't very old. And as the hours grew longer and the coughing louder and the night blacker, John curled up in a damp, smelly corner, and cried himself to sleep.

There was a rough iron grating in the hatch which let in a filter of light as the dawn came. Raking in his pocket for a few coins, John clambered across the sleeping bodies around him. Clinging to the grating he began to rattle them for all he was worth. A sailor above decks glanced down disinterestedly.

"You'll get your food."

"Take a message for me," John pleaded, holding a coin so that it glinted in the thin early morning sunlight. Cautiously the man came nearer to see if he was being fooled. Then he took the coin, turning it over in his hands, giving it a wrench with his teeth to see that it was sound.

"My name's Newton. Please help me," John kept on. "tell the Lieutenant I want to speak to him. Tell him. Please."

The man nodded his head, tossed the coin in his hand, shoved it into his pocket, and was gone without another glance in John's direction. Later, when some dry biscuits and tasteless gruel were passed down into the hold, and he crouched with the other men, eating by dim lantern light, John wondered whether the message would ever be given. And when he curled up in a slimy, smelly corner to sleep, he was still hungry.

The next day, when they were herded out on deck for exercise, tousled and blinking in the bright daylight, the Lieutenant strode up the gangplank and on board. Although John's damp clothes were spattered with mud and dirt, and his hair was tangled and filthy, he had an air of arrogance which caught the officer's eye.

"Newton!" he barked. "Which of you is Newton?" His eye ran through the tattered, sullen ranks lined up in front of him, and returned to John again. And John, stepping forward with his head held as high as he could, came to stand in front of him.

"I am, sir."

"What do you want?"

"My father is Captain Newton, sir. I'd like to send him a message so that he knows what has happened, sir."

"Where does he live?"

"Rotherhithe, sir." John daren't waste words, but at the same time, he was going to slip in the word "sir" as often as he could. Lieutenant Rubin didn't give him much chance.

"Very well." He turned to his Mate. "That's all. Take them back." The brief interview was over. "We sail tonight," John heard him say, as he was shuffled back to his gloomy quarters, to be pitched from his head to his heels as the little boat tossed on the last two days of its journey back to the *Harwich*.

John sat and waited in the depths of despair. The next few days were the worst jolt his pride had ever taken. On board the *Harwich* he was one of the lowest members of a crew of nearly four hundred. Pressganged sailors ranked below ordinary seamen. They were given the worst, dirtiest, heaviest tasks, crowded together, a hundred in a small space, with hardly any food. The air was so thick with filth, John felt he would choke before the ship set sail, and it was almost a relief to spend the days in the sun and the wind and the rain, scraping the masts of the ship, scraping her decks, and then, covered in icy spray, scraping and scraping until the sides of the boat were clean.

When at last Captain Cartaret of the *Harwich* received a letter from Captain Newton, he read it through several times. Then he laid it down on the table in front of him, and had John called to his cabin.

"You needn't think you'll be treated like a captain's son," he warned John sternly. "You'll get no privileges. But you'll get fairness. Clean yourself up, and get out on the quarter-deck. I'll have someone show you to your quarters. From now on, you take up duty as a midshipman."

It was lucky for John that the message arrived when it did, because the next morning the *Harwich* set sail.

2

DESERTING THE SHIP

THEY had just set sail when John heard the news.

"You know where we're going?" asked one of the ship's officers casually.

"Up and down the coasts—usual convoy stuff," John replied.

"Don't you believe it!" Then man laughed out loud. "Five years to the East Indies and back—you'd better say goodbye to your friends for a while!"

John stared at him. Five years! That was one of the longest voyages. And yet it was true.

They docked twice more before setting off. Each time, John was late back, because he galloped as fast as his horse could take him to Chatham where he stayed as many days as possible with a girl called Mary Catlett and her family, whom he loved as if they were his own family. And then he rode back again, having overstayed his leave. The first time, his friends covered up for him. The second time, he was summoned to the Captain's cabin and given double watch for the next three weeks.

"After all I've done for you," said Captain Cartaret, who was very angry. John winced at the words his father had used so many times. It never occurred to him to be grateful to the Captain. Without his kindness, John would still have been cramped and hounded with the rest of the conscripts. But he never said thank you. And he had no intention of saying he was sorry.

They were off the coast of Devon, heading for the open seas of the Atlantic, when he woke with a start one night. A storm was tossing the ship with such force that John's hammock had swung over and tipped him flat on his face on the floor. Up on deck, there was chaos as the wind smashed the lanterns and flames spluttered up and then died away, extinguished by the crash of waves on the deck. When morning came, the ship was so badly damaged that Captain Cartaret ordered an about turn, and they sailed quietly up Plymouth Sound to the boat-yards, to be made seaworthy before sailing off again for the East Indies.

John watched the shore. He felt strangely unsettled. He was so near dry land. It would be so easy to find his way back to Chatham and to Mary. So easy—because it looked so near. And yet it was the hardest thing for a sailor to cross that strip of water which separated the ship from land. Every hand was needed. On shore, men were still being caught and conscripted. Every ship was still short-handed. Every officer had his eyes skinned for deserters. It was impossible.

A seaman stood before John.

"Yes?"

"Captain's compliments, Mr. Newton. He wants you on deck."

John shrugged his shoulders and pulled himself

together. A few minutes later, he stood before the Captain.

"You know we're short-handed, Newton. I'm sending a ship ashore, and the men must be watched. Given half a chance, they'll desert. I want you to take it for me—see to it, will you?"

The next few minutes passed in a haze. The brisk marching of the men to the ropes and down on to the boat. The sharp commands to keep them from breaking ranks, The sight of the shore coming nearer and nearer. John's mind was in a turmoil. Faintly, he told himself he had a duty to do. But the excitement of a sudden chance of freedom was far too strong. The Captain had given him a chance, and he would be stupid not to take it. John had heard that his father was in Devon. If only he could reach him, and persuade him to help —to have his papers transferred and sign on perhaps for a shorter voyage on a merchant vessel. Even a vessel under his father's command. The ideas whirled wildly round in his head. As his feet touched dry land, all thoughts of duty disappeared. At first he walked, so as not to attract attention. Then he ran. And then, when he was far enough from sight of the *Harwich* where she lay anchored far out in the Sound, he walked again, not daring to ask the way or hire a horse, because every sailor out and alone, was suspected of desertion.

It was cold and starting to rain as John strode along the roads. It grew dark, but he kept on marching until the dawn came and the first birds began to sing. He was hungry, because there was no time to stop for food. And anyway, he had no money in his pocket. The Devon hills stretched out before him, all green and full of the promise of freedom. He whistled a little, quietly to himself. Then his whistling was interrupted by a shout.

"Halt!"

The road ended abruptly. If John had been watching more closely, he might have caught a glimpse of the scarlet coats of the soldiers waiting in a little group beyond the hedge. Now they were suddenly all around him, their muskets raised. John returned their gaze as levelly as he could.

"Where are you going?" The Lieutenant eyed John up and down, noting his midshipman's clothes, the tiredness behind the defiance in his eyes, and the faint catch of weariness and hunger in his voice.

"To meet my father, Captain Newton, before my ship HMS *Harwich* sails from the Sound."

Surprise registered in the soldier's eyes. For a moment there was silence, while he thought. John felt the hostility of the men around him, still keeping their rifles poised, with the barrels pointed straight at him.

"Where is your horse?"

John hesitated. He had never been any good at making up stories. "I couldn't hire one, sir."

The Lieutenant noticed less defiance in John's manner, and he seized on it.

"Where did you spend the night?"

"I, I . . ." For the life of him, John could think of no reply. The rifle butts came up eagerly. The Lieutenant sighed and signed to the men surrounding John.

"About turn!" A musket prodded him in the back, until he was heading back to Plymouth again.

Like a convict, they marched him back through the streets of Plymouth. The people in the roadside laughed at him and pointed. Some of them jeered. Others watched in sympathy. John hated them all. He hated anyone to see him being made to look stupid. He marched quickly with his head up and his eyes fixed straight in front of him. He was taken to a cold cell in the guard house while enquiries were made, and soldiers consulted their notes and wrote their reports, and entered his name in their long books of deserters rounded up as they made their way hopefully in from the sea to the roads that would have led them home.

Then he was marched out, and across the quay. He nearly burst out laughing when they hustled him into the little boat which he had commanded from the *Harwich* to the shore two days ago. Now his wrists were handcuffed together, and he had no power at all.

For a moment, the handcuffs were taken off to allow him to climb the ropes onto the *Harwich*. John could see the seamen on board stopping their work to watch him, with cold, curious eyes, as he was hustled on board. One of his friends passed by on his way to take the watch. John knew he had seen him, but the expression in his eyes didn't change, and he passed by without a word.

"Get a move on!" Someone shoved him from behind, and he was marched across the deck to the hatchway leading to the ship's hold.

The cold air hit him like a smack in the face as he was pushed down the iron rungs. The dampness and the smell reminded him of the days he had spent on board the *Betsey*, when they had first commandeered him at Deptford. In the brief swinging light of the lantern, he stumbled against the casks and crates stored for the long voyage. Then he felt the cold iron of the manacles snapped round his wrists again. The light of the lantern grew fainter as the footsteps grew fainter up the steps. There was a moment of daylight as the hatch lifted and closed again. Then pitch dark: the swaying of the ship letting water seep in between badly fitting boards; the gnawing of rats, searching for food; and the quick flicker of movement as a mouse ran across the floor.

John sat down and cried.

The darkness lasted a week. John didn't know it was a week. There was no way of telling night from day. Biscuits and water were brought to him, and by straining his ears, he could make out the sounds on deck. Vaguely he realized a day must have passed. And then another. There was an increase in the movement as sailing came slowly closer, and John lived in fear of spending an entire voyage crouched in irons, with only the rats to keep him company in the darkness. Then, one day, the routine changed. There was the sound of the bolts being drawn back, and footsteps approaching. In the swinging light of the lantern held by one of the sailors, John saw them making their way towards him. For the last week, no one had spoken to him. Now he was pulled to his feet.

"Take the irons off," the master-at-arms ordered the marines escorting him.

"Here," he held out clothes to John, when his hands were freed. "Put these on."

They were the vest and trousers of an ordinary seaman. John's wrists were so stiff that his hands shook trying to take off his dirty, damp clothes and handle the harsh material that was allowed to the lowest members of the crew. He was conscious of the eyes of the men ranged round him, waiting for him, noticing each hesitation, each weakness. He was aware of the mockery in their stare. Somehow defiance helped him to walk unassisted up the steel rungs into the daylight, where the sudden sun dazzled his eyes and made him stumble.

The entire ship's company was assembled on deck. He felt their eyes watching in curiosity as he was marched out before them all, into the middle of the deck. Then he was left standing alone, his feet bare beneath the wide bottomed trousers, the sun blazing down on his bare head. Nearly four hundred pairs of eyes were on him as Captain Cartaret stepped out of his cabin, looking doubly resplendent in his silk and ruffles, with his powdered wig and his silver sword.

In the silence, the charge was read out. And then the sentence. As he heard it, John nearly fainted. Gritting his teeth and clenching his hands until his fingernails made marks in his palms, he managed to remain standing quite still without showing a flicker of emotion.

He had been convicted of betrayal of trust and desertion. The punishment was eight dozen strokes of the cat. The cat was a whip made of thongs of tough leather. In the long, long silence, they took off John's shirt and chained him over a wooden bench. Then the punishment began.

One of the crew fainted. The rest had more admiration for John than for any other man on board. Somehow, by straining his nerves and using every ounce of will power he could find, he didn't cry out once. And when it was over, Captain Cartaret had to retire to his cabin and take a strong, stiff drink before his hands would stop shaking.

John didn't really know anything. In his mind, there was still the dull thud of the leather straps relentlessly on his back. He was still waiting for the renewed vigour with which each man attacked his task as they changed duties every dozen strokes. He didn't realize it was all over, and they were carrying him below decks to have his wounds sterilized with steaming alcohol, and rum forced between his lips.

He didn't see the ship's doctor bending over him, or hear him turn and ask wearily:

"Why didn't they hang him from the yard-arm and have done with it?"

3

"I WANT TO MAKE MY FORTUNE"

ROPES were being unfurled and chests tied together, ammunition stacked safely away in the hold. Crates of gunpowder followed hot on the heels of crates of thick, sweet wine. In the dim light of early morning, sailors staggered up the gangplank with great loads on their backs, as the *Harwich* made ready to sail from Madeira to the Cape of Good Hope.

John was still asleep in his hammock below decks.

He should have been up and dressed half an hour before, but the shrill sound of the pipes, and the shouts of the officers, and now even the banging and thudding of the loading and the screech of ropes as the sails were hoisted high to the top masts ready to catch the first breath of wind, failed to have any effect on him.

"Get up, you young fool!" shouted one of the sailors as he passed by.

"Go away," muttered John, his eyes still closed.

But the man had already gone, scuttling off to his duties as a midshipman appeared down the hatch. He was one of John's old friends. He strode straight to the only hammock still slung across the men's quarters.

"Newton!" He shook the hammock roughly, and John opened his eyes. "Get up on deck at once—and you can take double duties."

John shut his eyes again.

Impatiently, the officer pulled his knife from his belt. In one quick movement he cut through the ropes suspending the hammock from the wooden cross beams. Then he strode off leaving John in a heap on the floor.

Slowly he disentangled himself. Then he began to dress. Slowly still. Sullenly. Seething with anger that someone who had once been his friend could make such a fool of him.

The scars on his back still made him wince when he ran the cold water over them, and then again when he put on his shirt. Before they had properly healed, he had been forced to climb to the topmost rigging and when he had swayed there, sick with pain and dizzy with weakness, they had laughed at him for being afraid.

"I'll kill him!" he swore to himself a hundred times a day, watching Captain Cartaret striding the quarter deck. At night, he dreamed about it. And out on watch, gazing into the ceaseless movement of the waves he swore he would throw himself over the side, to drown or be eaten by sharks.

It never occurred to him that the treatment given to him by the midshipmen who had once been his friends was no harsher than he had given when he had held the same position. It never occurred to him that if he had been more kind to the ordinary seamen under him, they might have been more kind to him now. Instead, he swore and fought and quarrelled, broke the rules and tried to evade his duties. If it hadn't been for the thought of Mary, untouched by it all at her home in Chatham, he would have carried out his wildest dreams and killed himself or the Captain, but at the thought of her, his voice softened, and his tongue stumbled on the swear words, and he kept doggedly on.

Walking defiantly slowly, he wandered up on deck. The early morning sun had just pierced the mist, and the screeching of brilliant birds echoed from palm tree to palm tree. There were other ships at anchor, swaying softly in the slight waves that lapped gently on the white sands. There were graceful shining ships, glinting gold and gilt in the sun, making their passage from Spain with spices and oils and silks on board. There were tea clippers, thin and fragile, bringing their cargo back from the East Indies, and barques with their holds full of chests of tobacco and cotton from South America, where slaves from Africa worked to supply the sudden demand from the West, as the new fashion for smoking in long clay pipes spread through the aristocracy. And there were the slave ships themselves, called Guinea ships, because they picked up their cargo along the Guinea coasts before setting off on the Middle Passage from Africa to the West Indies and America, where they swopped their living cargo for a hold full of cotton and sugar, tobacco and rum. John had never been on board a slaver, but he had watched the seamen loading on crates of manacles and iron collars to keep the slaves in order during the long voyages.

The sight was as commonplace as the loading and unloading of any cargo.

For a moment John stood there watching it all, surrounded by the bustle and clatter of a ship preparing to sail. He was turning to take his disgruntled part in the work, as a man pushed past him, clutching a bundle of clothes under his arm.

"You decided to get up, then!" It was the sailor who had tried to rouse him earlier.

"What are you doing?" asked John, curiously. "Where are you going?"

The man didn't stop. He was running to the side of the deck, where a rowing boat waited below. He threw his clothes down, and then swung himself over the side to begin the descent down the rope ladder. John stared in astonishment. Then he ran across the deck after him.

"It's the Guinea ship," the man called up to him. "They wanted an exchange—two for two." Waving triumphantly to John, he jumped into the boat, and pulled away towards the cumbersome slaver anchored further out at sea.

John didn't stop to watch.

"Two for two!" That meant the Guinea ship had another place on board. Swallowing his pride, John ran to the cabin of the Lieutenant who had first forced him into service on the *Harwich*.

"Please let me go to the Guinea ship," he begged, close to tears in his desperation. "Please, sir. They want another man, and—" his mind searched wildly for something to weigh in his favour, "and they have a first-class carpenter to exchange in his place."

"Third-class anything would be better than another Newton on board," retorted the Lieutenant sourly. "Get your things by all means. I'm glad to see the back of you." And in spite of the ungraciousness of his dismissal, John nearly went down on his knees he was so thankful.

His hands shaking with relief and excitement, he climbed down the hatch and collected together his few belongings. The paper he kept always with him for writing letters to Mary. The tattered waterproof leather wallet in which he kept his little money and the few short letters she had written to him, stilted and correct. A change of clothes, and some books. Elements of Geometry by Euclid, the philosopher from ancient Greece, which fascinated John with its neat, precise diagrams and its sense of discovery and adventure; and books of Latin which he translated piece by piece, identifying himself as he sailed round the world with Vergil's mythical Ulysses. The few things didn't make a very large bundle. John tied them all up in a spare shirt, found himself a boat to take him across to the ship, and, without a backward glance at anyone, he was away.

For the first time since they docked at Madeira, he noticed the way the sunshine shaded the dark and light of the palm trees. He saw the sudden flash of scarlet wings through blue sky, and he felt a warm tinge of happiness. For the first time in months, life seemed to be worth living.

As the gap widened between him and the *Harwich*, John marvelled at coincidence. The coincidence which had made the midshipman angry enough to cut down his hammock and force him up on deck in time to see the rowing boat setting out. But coincidence didn't fit in to John's new way, the way of a thinking man who could explain everything. And so he pushed it to the back of his mind, gathered up his bundle, and prepared to climb aboard the great slaver, towering above him.

He was determined to trust no one, in case they made a fool of him. With no friends to keep and no promises to break, he could be as wild and as bad as he liked. He was really going to enjoy himself.

The Captain of the *Pegasus* was a tough stern man. He prided himself on being a disciplinarian, which meant he was tough on the slaves when he took them on board, and tough on his own crew all the time.

In those days in England, it was a respectable thing to captain a slave ship. The slave trade was looked upon much like any other trade. The fact that it was inhuman, cruel and wrong was lost sight of in the glories and the gold that could be found by trading a good cargo of slaves for a hold full of cotton and rum. That women died and boys jumped overboard and men had to be forced to eat food because they would rather starve than stay alive, was explained away with a wave of the hand and a purse of gold coins, and no one bothered to enquire any further. "It saves them from something far worse," they said vaguely. But no one ever knew what.

John vaguely remembered his father talking of the slave run, and the ships that tacked up and down the coasts, bartering people for goods. Now he would see for himself.

No one took much notice of him that first morning, as he boarded the ship, clutching his papers and his belongings.

"Newton." The Captain glanced at the boy. "No relation to Captain Newton, of course,' he added, hardly waiting for an answer.

"He's my father, sir," John told him politely.

The Captain ran his eye over John's papers. "Insubordination ... desertion ... abuse ... evading duties ..." Then he looked up again at the boy standing before him, his hair bleached like straw and his square face tanned brown by the wind and the sun, barefoot, and wearing the soiled vest and wide trousers of a common sailor.

"He must be proud of you, I'm sure," he remarked tartly. "All right, get off to your duties and be sharp about it. I'll have none of that aboard my ship."

John turned on his heel and marched away, and the Captain winced as the words this new charge was muttering under his breath were carried behind him on the breeze. He shook his head. "I'm going to have trouble there," he told himself.

*   *   *

"You're a new face, lad!" John looked up, startled to hear the loud, north country voice. "You look a bright one. I've heard your talk too. That's bright. Who are you?"

"Newton, sir." John had seen him before,

strutting round the ship, dining at the Captain's table, and given the best of everything. He had a red face and bright, brash, rich clothes, with large gold buckles on his shoes.

"Newton? You're Captain Newton's son, then."

"Yes, sir."

Amos Clow had heard about John Newton. He had heard something of his wild background. "At least," he thought looking at John, "he has spirit." He was quite impressed.

John was even more impressed by the stories he heard that night over supper.

"Clow!" The whistles and the winks. "Hadn't a penny three years ago—then . . ." The snapped fingers. The admiration. "Of course you know why he's on this ship?"

John shook his head.

"He owns a quarter share in it. That's why. He's got a reputation the length of the Coast for driving a hard bargain and getting good money." A hundred, said one. A thousand, argued another. Ten thousand! The fortune of gold pieces grew bigger with each tale. In three years, Clow had made more money than any other man from his dealings in the slave trade.

That night, alone on watch, John was deep in thought. Was it really so easy to make a fortune? In his imagination, he knelt before Mary, asking her to marry him and tipping out pockets full of gleaming gold coins before her astonished eyes. They would all admire him—Lieutenant Rubin, Captain Cartaret, the midshipmen and the mates. Even his father.

The next morning, John went in search of Clow, but they had dropped anchor at first light, and he had gone ashore to barter for the first consignment of slaves down the long coastal journey. All around John, the boxes of irons were being opened and thrown out on the decks, counted and sorted ready into two's. Several hours later, the first boatload was hustled on board, and John watched, with curious, not very interested eyes.

What he saw horrified him.

Women and children were pushed to one side of the ship. Men to the other. They cowered there like frightened animals, while their wrists were manacled and their ankles chained two by two. Then they were taken, some sobbing and crying, some silent and afraid, to their quarters below decks. Quarters too low to stand up in, and too cramped to move.

"There's a good one." John turned. Amos Clow fingered his silk ruffled shirt, and pointed out one of the men with satisfaction. "Got him for a dud barrel of powder and a rusted musket!" He roared with laughter. "Oil him until his skin shines, and he'll fetch a good price in the South."

The mention of money made John forget the sickness he had felt at his first sight of the slaves. "Mr. Clow, sir," he began cautiously.

The big, red-faced man turned to him.

"Mr. Clow, sir, please, I wish you'd take me into service with you. I'd work hard, sir, I swear I would," he added quickly as he saw a frown coming on the older man's face. "I know all there is to know about ships and the sea, sir, and I'm handy with money. And I want to make my fortune, too, Sir."

The last remark flattered Mr. Clow. He was proud of the money he had made, and he liked to hear it talked about.

"You're right, lad," he beamed. "I've done well." He wasn't a man to mince words. "I've done well," he repeated, because he liked people to know. "Not without hard graft though," he added, nodding sternly at John. "I don't fool around. I don't waste time. I get on with a job."

For the second time in his life, John felt like getting down on his knees. "I'll work hard, Mr. Clow. I'll work harder than I've ever worked before. And I'm tough." His mind went back to the flogging. "I can stand any amount of hardship and pain. I'll be indispensable to you," he added desperately, taking a leaf out of Mr. Clow's boastful book.

"How old are you, lad?"

"Nineteen."

Mr. Clow's eyes narrowed. For a moment John wondered when he had seen that look before. Then he remembered. It was when the slaver was studying his haul of slaves being herded down below decks. Now he looked John up and down in the same way, taking in his height, his strength his strong arms, straight back, and wilful, adventurous eyes.

"Very well. I'll see what I can do."

John ran back to his duties beside himself with excitement.

Amos Clow made his way back to his cabin to draft out a letter to the Captain legalizing John's discharge. He was pleased with himself. He had struck a good bargain. He always did.

4

ON THE SLAVE COAST

"WHO is this?"
The voice was imperious and harsh. And yet it had a charm. John looked up. A beautiful woman with dark skin and dark black eyes was holding Amos Clow's arm. There were coloured bangles on her ankles and arms. She was wearing a dress of brilliant silk which John had seen Clow bargaining for along the coast. Now she pulled her arm from his and repeated the question angrily.

"Who is this boy?"

John stood up. His hands felt large and cumbersome, and he was aware that his jaw was too big and square. He dropped his eyes awkwardly under the woman's scorching gaze. And for a moment, in spite of the warm sunshine and the green sea like glass lapping round the tiny island, he felt a cold shiver of fear down the back of his neck.

Clow roared with laughter.

"The two most important people in my life!" he joked. He stuck his hand out towards John. "John Newton, late of His Majesty's Royal Navy, late of the Guinea ship *Pegasus*, now employed by the great Coral Coast tycoon Amos Clow, as first mate, right-hand man, assistant and friend!" He performed a mock bow with great flourish and ceremony.

"John," he continued, his tone softer. "Meet my beautiful island wife."

In his astonishment and confusion, John hardly heard the name of Clow's wife. It sounded like two initials, P.I., and since he never learned how to spell her name properly in all the days that followed, they stuck in his mind as a kind of nickname.

One thing he knew without a shadow of doubt. P.I. didn't like him.

The tiny island was the smallest of a group called the Plantanes, set in the green seas of the Gulf of Guinea. From the farthest tip, called Shilling Point, John could strain his eyes and see the Banana Islands. From the near side of the island, the two larger Plantanes rose like dark hummocks in the hazy sun, and the breeze whispering through the palm trees mingled with the gentle lapping of the water and the sudden flick of a silver fish, or the cackle of a bird darting across the sky.

Amos Clow had already established himself on the other islands. He had bases where men working for him took long thin boats out up the coasts and into the dangerous creeks where sharks snapped at the oars and natives threw poisoned darts. The men made frequent lightning journeys up the creeks, to snatch men and women and children from the villages far inland, binding them hand and foot and bringing them back to fetch a good price from the slave ships as they stopped on their way to America.

Amos Clow was proud of his business. He

made a lot of money. And like so many people who make a lot of money, it made him want to make a lot more. So he and John began building a third house on this tiny island, no more than two miles from one end to the other. From there, he would train John to sail the long boats up dangerous parts of the coast as yet unknown and un-explored.

"When will I earn some money for myself, Mr. Clow, sir?" asked John tentatively one day, as they packed mud on to the roof of the straw thatch, where it would bake hard and dry in the sun.

"What's that?"

John was sure he had heard, but he was determined to press the point.

"Money, sir. I wondered when you might be paying me some money."

"Wait until the next ship calls, lad. There'll be money enough for us both and to spare." He swept the question aside. 'But you get now't without working for it, you know.'

John did know. He was working hard from early morning until the sudden night came and the moonflowers opened and the crickets began to chirrup in the dark. But he was happy. He could do near enough as he liked. There was no one to tell him to sluice the decks or be back by nightfall or say his prayers. He could use as many bad words as he liked, and when he did, it gave him a kind of satisfaction. It made him feel big and grown up.

Amos Clow didn't care. "Curse whoever you like, lad, so long as you don't curse me. And do what you like, so long as you do your work."

At night, they slept in huts until the house was

finished, and, although John haughtily ignored the servants Clow employed from the neighbouring islands, he heard their tales of the leopard men who caught strangers at night, and ate them alive. He laughed as loudly as Clow at the stories.

"Stupid fools!" he sneered, and Clow joined him, laughing loudly. But when it was dark, and John tumbled exhausted on to his bed of straw, thankful for a few hours' relief from the burning heat of the sun on his back as he worked, the rustling in the trees kept him awake. And sometimes, when he heard a sound like the sound of footsteps and breathing near the door of his hut, he leaped up, feeling for his knife. But it was only P.I., walking around softly, almost silently, seeing that all was well.

"You look frightened, Mr. Newton," she said to him gently, in her perfect, stilted English. "What can have made you so pale?"

And when he could think of no reply but to walk sheepishly back to his bed and lie down, her beautiful face came into dreams that turned into nightmares. She was always smiling. But to John, it seemed a very mocking smile.

It was nearly Christmas before the house was finished. On Christmas Eve, there was to be a grand banquet—which made John laugh, because although there would be a dozen servants to do the work, only three people would sit down to supper. Nevertheless, it was to be a grand occasion.

It was a great day for P.I. She had prepared enormous bowls full of food, some of it island delicacies, but the majority cooked as Clow liked it cooked, with a little of all that was best from every place he had ever been to round the world. The bowls were highly polished silver and gold, and instead of her coloured bangles, P.I. wore thick circles of solid gold, jangling on her arms.

John and Amos Clow drank a lot between them, and began singing uproarious carols, with the words all jumbled up and out of tune.

"You're a good lad!" Clow reached across the table and shook John's hand enthusiastically. And John was aware of P.I.'s eyes turned to him, blazing with jealousy.

For a moment he felt on fire himself He reached for some water, and the sudden coolness of it made his hands shiver. It was always cold at night in the tropics, he told himself But the coldness seemed to spread through him, and he had to drink again before he could bring himself to begin eating the next heaped plateful put in front of him.

"Very good," muttered Clow, eating his way through the food at a great rate. P.I. preened herself.

"It was always your favourite dish. You see, I remembered. It was when we dined together at ..."

Clow interrupted her. He wasn't listening. "Sing us another, Newton!" he said, his eyes fixed eagerly on John. "You've a good voice, and a good wit too. You can make me laugh."

John stood up. He didn't know why he stood up, except that the heat seemed suddenly unbearable, and P.I.'s silent anger was unbearable, and he just wanted to be outside where the water was cool and green and he could walk with Mary under the palm trees. He shook himself. Surely he was dreaming. Mary was at home. And yet everything seemed unreal: the silver and gold plates, swimming with reflected faces, all out of shape, distorted and weird. He stood there, hanging on to the edge of the table to steady himself, shivering with cold and burning with heat, seeing P.I.'s face, her mocking smile, her fiery anger and sullen jealousy, staring at him everywhere he looked.

Then he fainted.

"Of course," remarked Clow, standing by his bedside a few days later, "they all catch the fever at first. But they get over it."

But John didn't hear. He couldn't really hear anything. There was just the day and the night, and heat and icy coldness which didn't seem to bear any relation to sunshine or darkness. Sometimes he heard a voice calling out for water, and he wondered who it belonged to. And when they heard him calling, and brought him water, and pressed it between his lips, the heat in his body seemed to dry it up before it had a chance to refresh him.

"Just when I needed help!" grumbled Amos Clow, watching John tossing and turning on his bed. "Now I'll have to make the first trip inland without him." He fretted and fumed, and John was vaguely conscious of his voice angrily cursing "good-for-nothing weaklings from the South". Then he stamped off out, and there was silence. For a moment, John was aware of the relief that came with being alone. And then the fever and the sickness and the aching in his head took over, and he was aware of very little else.

He didn't see Clow and P.I. standing in the doorway watching him, as Clow prepared to set out on his long trip. He didn't hear Clow talking to his wife in hushed tones.

"Take care of him," he repeated to her. "Give him water until the fever turns, and then food, a little at a time, until he can take more." She nodded carefully, smiling up at him.

"I want him well when I return," were Clow's last words, as he set off with the bearers marching in front of him, armed with spears to ward off sharks, and with charms round their necks, to ward off the evil spells of the leopard men. "He will be of great use to me. I need him."

The smile faded on P.I.'s face. But the trader had gone. He wouldn't be home for months. P.I. turned and went back into the house. Now she was alone. She could do as she liked. She called two of her servants, and discussed with them the rich, elaborate dinner she would eat that evening. Then she went to her room to dream about the ivory and silks her English husband might bring back for her, as well as villagers in chains.

John tossed and turned. He could hear buzzing in his ears, filling his head, like an army of hungry mosquitoes. But when he opened his eyes, there was nothing there. And the light made his eyes ache. Outside, the sun reached its height, and then began slowly sinking. John's throat burned drier and drier. He heard the strange voice which must be his own and yet seemed to belong to someone else far away, calling and calling for water.

But no one came.

5

FEVER-STRICKEN ISLAND

JOHN opened his eyes. He had no idea where he was, or how long he had been unconscious. His body ached and his head hurt. It was very dark. He moved slightly, and was aware of the hardness of the bed beneath him.

Gradually his eyes grew more accustomed to the darkness. Through the open timber doorway, he could hear the rustle of the leaves, and the first filtering light as the dawn came.

He was in the hut which had been his makeshift home while the house was built. His bed was a rush mat spread on a hard wooden chest. A log of wood had been placed under his head as a pillow. Slowly, slowly, he began to remember. But the hardness of the wood made his head ache, and he shut his eyes and tried to sleep again.

The only thing he could remember clearly was his raging thirst, and the longing for water. And as he became more conscious, the thirst returned. It became so strong that he couldn't sleep. Outside the door, the sun rose higher in the sky, and the breeze died down in the leaves. There wasn't a sound except for the sudden whirr of wings and chatter of noise as a bird flew through the trees. It must be noon, with the leaves hanging dry and hot in the sun, without a whisper of wind anywhere.

"Water!"

John's lips were so parched and dry that his voice seemed to crack. The fever had left him so weak that he couldn't call very loudly.

"Water!" he called, again and again, but there wasn't a sound outside, and no one came. Desperately he summoned what strength he had to roll himself off the hard wooden bed, and begin crawling slowly and painfully on all fours towards the door. When he had almost reached the opening, he lay for a moment on the floor, too exhausted to go on, feeling the slight freshness of the air beyond the hut cooling his forehead and his hot eyes. As he lay there, there was a movement outside. A black face and two bright eyes peered nervously round the door. Strong arms lifted him and helped him back to the rough bed. Then he felt something hard pressed to his lips, and tears of relief filled his eyes. He was being given water.

A moment later, he was alone.

The next few days passed in the same way. The slaves he had laughed at and poked fun at were now risking their safety to keep him alive. First one, and then another, would slip in against the shadowy wall, and give him a little of their small ration of water or rice. Rather than satisfying his thirst and hunger, it made John long for more food, for more to drink. But at least it kept him alive.

Then one day P.I. herself came in to have a look at her prisoner.

She gazed down at him, smiling as always. "So you are well again," she said, mockingly. "And still idling in bed."

"If you would give me some food, I might be strong enough to get out of bed," John replied wearily.

"We'll see," she said tartly, and went away.

That night, she sent John her own silver plate. He struggled up hungrily, the thought of food turning his tummy over with excitement. He didn't care that all she had left were the bones from her chicken and the last remnants of the rice which she couldn't eat herself. He gnawed the left-overs until the bones were bare and shining. It was hardly enough to take the edge off his hunger, but it was something.

The next morning, she came early to the hut. She had with her the slaves who had been bringing John their own food. Now, instead of looking at him in pity, their eyes were on the ground, avoiding him, waiting to do whatever she told them.

"Well?" She stood over him. "I have given you food. Now you must get out of bed. You have been lazy for long enough."

John looked up at her in amazement.

"Come on!" she hurried him. "If you want food, get up and walk for it."

Slowly, John pulled himself off the bed. His legs felt shaky and weak as they touched the hard mud floor of the hut. He pulled himself up, gripping onto the side of the hard wooden chest. Then he began to totter unsteadily towards the door.

P.I. threw back her head and laughed. It was a shrill, piercing sound like the coarse calling of the peacocks at dawn. The sound went round and round in John's head, and he swayed slightly, but forced himself to go on walking resolutely towards the door.

"Such a marvellous fellow, and he can't even walk properly!" P.I. laughed and laughed. "Copy him!" she commanded the slaves, huddled nervously in the doorway. They hesitated. "I wish to be amused," she commanded them angrily. "Copy the white man."

Slowly the slaves fell into step behind John, imitating his tottering footsteps, swaying when he swayed, stumbling when he stumbled, groping blindly for the wall to steady themselves, as he did. John felt tears of humiliation and rage stinging his eyes. But he had to keep on. He knew he was so weak that he was totally in P.I.'s power. And if he had no food, he would die. He didn't hear P.I. whispering to one of the slaves, and sending him outside. As John reached the door of the hut, he felt something hard hit his arm. Then his leg and his shoulder. He was being pelted with hard green limes. And behind him, P.I. laughed and laughed, and told the slaves to laugh too. Then she left him alone.

To John's relief, she didn't visit him again for over a week. He was sent small rations of rice and water, just enough to keep him alive. But he was still very, very hungry. Then one day, she sent for him. She was sitting at the long table where their Christmas banquet had been held. Plates and bowls were heaped high with food. The sight of it made John faint with hunger.

Once again, she was handing him the left-overs from her own dish, and although he hated himself for it, he thanked her, with tears in his eyes. But as she gave him the plate, it was so heavy, and John's hands so weak, that he dropped it on the floor. The precious gravy ran in rivulets and disappeared. He knelt down and tried to scoop it up with his hands, but it was no good.

"Give me some more," he begged, his eyes wandering from dish to dish on the piled table. But she just laughed.

"You should be more careful," she said.

That night, John was so hungry that he stole out of the hut and made his way to the plantation where young lime saplings were being planted out, to add to the income Amos Clow already had from coconuts and rice. In a frenzy of hunger and desperation, he pulled up root after root and chewed the bitter, tough stalks. For a moment, he was satisfied. Then he went back to the hut, tired out, and before he went to sleep, he was violently sick.

When Amos Clow came home, he said that the fever made men suffer from all kinds of hallucinations.

"We'll soon have you strong again," he told John, his arm round P.I. He waved aside John's accusations. "I know, I know," he said, as if he was speaking to a child. "We all imagine things when we're ill."

"He is a lazy boy," remarked P.I. flatly.

"Surely not." Clow was reluctant to accept his wife's assessment of John's value. But he obviously did not dismiss it altogether. "We shall soon see about that," he said. "As soon as you're well, lad, I'm off on another trip up river. And you're coming too."

John was overjoyed at the thought of a few months away from P.I. He was being given more food now, because P.I. had no intention that her husband should have the slightest inkling how she had treated John while he was away. Gradually John felt his strength returning. One day he was taking enough interest in life to clip his long beard neatly round his chin, and to notice that a little of the old tan was returning to his pale cheeks.

The day they set off together in the long, open boat, with provisions enough for several months and beads and wines, guns and flints, gunpowder, silks and knives, to pay their way, John felt almost well enough to look forward to the trip with pleasure. It was a new adventure.

"You look better, lad." Amos Clow was feeling very friendly towards John. He was sure P.I. was wrong when she said John was lazy and dishonest. He looked at the boy. His face was still lined with the severity of his illness, but it had matured and toughened a lot over the last few months. Clow smiled at him.

"We're going to do well, this trip. We'll make good partners," he said, opening one of the bottles of wine loaded for bartering. "It's bad wine," he said.

"You mean we barter with bad wine?" asked John innocently.

Clow laughed loudly. "You don't waste good

wine up river," he said. "These fools don't know the difference between good and bad wine. They don't know a damp keg of powder or a dud flint. So why waste them?"

Slowly they slipped up the coast, nosing round the rocks shimmering just below the surface of the clear waters, and charging the foaming rapids of the inland streams as they cascaded down to the sea. Once an inquisitive shark snapped off the head of one of the native's oars, and he swore it was the evil influence of the leopard man.

The first stop they made, John captured two women in exchange for some silks. Clow was very pleased with him. They set off further inland, and John looked forward to the next village. He was enjoying himself.

There was another trader already established in the village when they arrived with their train of native bearers and tempting offers. He and Clow welcomed each other. They were both Europeans, and they knew each other well. John disliked the sharp, mean look in the stranger's eyes, but he went off to begin his business without giving it any more thought. When he returned to the boat that night, Clow was waiting for him.

"So you've got the nerve to come back again, you scoundrel!" John's mouth dropped open. Clow's face grew redder and redder as he grew more angry. "You take my food and my hospitality. You slander my wife, and laze around like a good-for-nothing. Then when I take you with me and give you the chance to earn some money for yourself, you cheat me!"

"But I—" John began.

"Shut your mouth! I don't want to hear your lies. If it hadn't been for the sharp sight of the friend I met this morning, you might have got away with it. I might have believed you. But he saw you. So there's nothing you can say."

"What have I done?" John shouted above the steady stream of abuse that was being poured out at him. "What am I supposed to have done?"

"*Supposed* to have done? I'll tell you what you're supposed to have done. There are three bales of silk and a cask of rum missing from the load. They happened to disappear about the same time that you went off into the forest towards the village."

"The same time your 'friend' left this ship," muttered John, but Clow was so beside himself that he didn't hear.

"They are now in the hut belonging to the local Chief," he went on, spluttering with indignation that anyone should have managed to outwit him. "And he says they were sold to him for money by a white trader."

Clow didn't speak to John any more. He made the slaves fasten a long chain to his leg and secure it to the upper deck. "Thief—ungrateful thief!" he muttered whenever he came near. And John's protests that he was innocent fell on ears as deaf as the hard rocks beneath the sea.

"P.I. was right," John heard Clow say to himself one day. "I should have listened to her. She was right."

And when he went ashore trading, he left John a prisoner on deck for days on end, with hardly any food and no protection from the heat or the heavy spray from the sea.

At first, the sun was so hot that John longed to be able to reach the shade where the hatchway led down below the deck. But the chain on his ankle wasn't long enough. His shirt and trousers were threadbare, and he forced himself to keep walking up and down so that the sun didn't seem to beat down quite so relentlessly. Then the weather changed. The nights grew cold, and the sun began to lose its strength. One morning, the rains came. Great hailstones, hard and icy cold. John managed to steal a length of cotton which he tied round his shoulders like a shirt, and an old handkerchief which he had taken to keep the sun from beating down on his head. It was soon sodden through and torn in shreds by the wind. The gales tossed and tore at the ship, and the salt stung John's eyes, and he longed for a sight of the sun again, however unbearably hot it felt.

Now, for the second time, he was aware of the pity in the black eyes of the slaves, as they went silently about their duties on the tossing ship. One day, he begged some pieces of chicken liver from them. Making himself a rough rod and line, he fastened the meat to the end. The slaves watched him in fascination, wondering what he was going to do. Patiently, John sat with his line ready, while the boat tossed and spun in the height of the gale. The tide was low, and the current from the fast flowing river made the water like a whirlpool.

Then, towards noon, when the tide was high, the waters calmed. His hands trembling in his effort to hurry and make the most of the few precious hours, John cast the line over the side of the ship. Within half an hour, he had caught three fish.

"Cook fishes?" suggested one of the slaves, shyly, knowing Clow would kill him if he came back and found him helping John.

"Yes—yes, please!" John's mouth was watering so much that he could hardly speak. And when the three fishes were cooked, smoking and crisp, it seemed like a feast.

Luckily John was a good fisherman. With his daily allowance of a pint of rice, and the few fish he managed to catch when the tide was high and the fast threshing current of the river was running more smoothly, he managed to keep alive.

There was only one thing he dreaded more than the hatred in Amos Clow's face. That was the gloating pleasure which he knew would fill P.I.'s face, when they returned to the island, and she was able to say to her husband, "I told you so!"

* * *

There were hundreds of limes to be planted before the rains ended and the hot sun came again, to draw the young plants upwards to the light. Mechanically John did the work. Digging the hole with his hands, the soft sandy earth filling his finger-nails. Then the plant. One plant after another after another, in long straight rows. He kept his eyes on what he was doing. If he looked up, the rows seemed to go on for ever.

Sometimes he thought of Mary. She would be 19 now. She was probably married, or dancing every night with young men with money, handsome young men, with good positions in the City.

He didn't dream any more about revenge or money or being bolder than anyone else. There didn't seem to be anything left to dream about. To be a slave bought on the island from the island villages, was bad enough. To be a white slave owned by a white master was worse.

The sand flew in all directions as John dug and dug. And slowly the rows of new, fresh green lime trees marched like toy soldiers across the island.

He didn't hear P.I. and Amos Clow coming up behind him,, as they strolled round one evening, inspecting the work on the plantations.

"Why, here's your assistant!" The harsh, sarcastic voice made John jump. But he went on, resolutely digging and planting, digging and planting.

Clow laughed. He kicked over one of the seedlings John had just planted. "One day, when you're captain of a fine ship, you can come and pick limes!" he said.

And they went off together, laughing at such a funny joke, while John turned back patiently and began to replant the broken seedling.

6

SMUGGLING THE LETTER

SOMETIMES ships bound for England stopped at the islands. When that happened, John ran away and hid in the woods. He hated the way the sailors pointed at him and laughed at him. They had never seen an English slave before.

But one day he joined Clow's servants rowing the boat out to a ship anchored beyond the rocks. He had a tightly folded piece of paper in his hand. Before the unloading was finished, he had persuaded one of the seamen on board the English ship to take a letter home with him.

It was addressed to Captain Newton.

John had found the paper between the pages of his book of Euclid. The thin sheet had become brittle with the heat. Amos Clow had given it to John more than a year ago, when they had been planning how to divide work on the estate between them. It had lain there, forgotten and untouched during John's fever, and the unhappy journey up river. Then one day, as a flicker of interest arose in John's mind, he had found the book, wondering if it might be worth studying. The paper had fluttered out as he turned the pages. Using a sharpened quill from the feather of a sea bird, which he picked up from the sand, and a mixture of dye from the barks of the trees in the forest, he had written a letter to his father.

He didn't say he was sorry. He didn't say he was working as a slave. John still had a lot of pride, in spite of everything that had happened.

"If you want me home," he wrote, "I will gladly come. Although I cannot imagine how."

And for John, the words showed a great deal of humility.

They rowed back from the ship, in and out of the rings of jagged rocks. When they landed, while the slaves dragged the boat up on to the sand, John went off by himself, climbing to the height of the island, and then down again, where the rocks dropped sharply to form small shady coves. It was quiet, with only the sound of the sea lapping quietly on the deserted beach. John took off his shirt, and washed it in the clear water. Then he spread it out on a boulder to dry, stiff and hard in the sun. That done, he settled down to the pastime which had become a kind of escape.

With a long stick he traced a triangle in the sand. One side twice the length of the other. Then the third. John smiled to himself. It worked. Thoughtfully he turned the next page in Euclid's book of elementary mathematics.

The sun was high in the sky, and the rocks surrounding the tiny sandy cove sent black shadows across the yellow sand. Carefully John studied the next proposition, worked out by the Greek mathematician years and years ago.

There were still a couple of hours before he was due to begin work on the plantation. He could study two more pages by then. He glanced back. He had completed the three first stages of the fascinating textbook since the rains had ended. He squatted down to pore over the next set of diagrams, his bare back brown, except for the white marks where the cat-o'-nine-tails had left long scars. He was glad some quirk of fate had made him keep the worn book with him. The hours he spent with it, when he could creep away by himself, gave him a sense of adventure and pleasure which he had forgotten existed.

He picked up the long pointed stick, and began slowly tracing another complicated figure in the sand.

"I never got that far with Euclid, myself." The man had come up behind John, who was concentrating so hard he neither saw nor heard him. The sun, shining directly down on John, threw the man's shadow behind him.

"You must be Mr. Newton."

Slowly, John looked up, hardly able to believe his ears. It was months since anyone had addressed him with any kind of courtesy. To his astonishment, this man, middle-aged and well-dressed, was holding out his hand.

"How do you like it here?" he asked, with a quizzical smile on his face.

"I don't like it. I hate it, sir." The words came out hesitantly. It was a long time since John had carried on a conversation with anyone. Now it was an effort, and he was shy. He was more shy than ever as he became uncomfortably aware of his bare back and his bare feet, and the ragged trousers, torn and faded in the sun.

"Why don't you work for me?"

John raised his eyes. "But Mr. Clow . . ."

"I've spoken to Clow. I don't agree with anyone who keeps a man as he is keeping you. He'll let you go. He tells me," he went on, watching John closely, "that you are a thief and a liar."

"I give you my word that I am neither, sir," replied John. For a moment their eyes met.

"I trust you," said the man. "And I've never trusted Clow."

His name was Williams. He had been a passenger on the English ship now sailing on up the coast. Like Clow, he was a trader, and, if John worked well for him, he promised him the management of his factory further up the mainland, storing goods for barter, and receiving, housing and sending out the slaves as they were brought from the inland raids and then sent off in shiploads to America. It was a responsible job, and John couldn't believe his luck.

*   *   *

They had hardly landed at the base, and begun unloading the vast cargo of goods to be stored ready for trading up the river in return for slaves, when John heard his name called out.

"John Newton!"

He must be dreaming. No one knew him on the Guinea Coast—no one but Williams and Clow.

"John Newton! Has anyone seen a white man called John Newton?"

John couldn't see who it was shouting. He pushed past a knot of sailors heaving a chest on to their backs, and shaded his eyes against the sun.

"John Newton!"

Now he could see who it was. It was a tall, distinguished man, dressed in the fashionable clothes of a rich trader from England. He wore a large three-cornered cockaded hat, and his eyes were the straight, blue eyes of a man who had spent his life at sea. For a moment, John hesitated. England seemed so far away. Mr. Williams had promised him adventure. Perhaps even a fortune. In a year or two he might be as rich as Amos Clow. And after so long, the thought of England frightened him a little.

Then someone caught the man's arm and pointed towards John.

"John!" He came striding across, his hands held out. "Your father asked me to try to find you. My name is Manesty—Captain Manesty of the *Greyhound*." He was smiling, and he had humorous eyes.

The letter, written so hastily on thin, soiled paper, had reached home.

7

THE VOICE IN THE STORM

A stiff gale was blowing up as the *Greyhound* left Newfoundland.

"There are storms ahead." The first mate looked worried. He and John studied the sky, watching the dark clouds gathering as night fell. "I don't like the look of it. We're in no condition to take a beating."

Shrugging his shoulders, John went to his cabin to spend the evening reading one of the few books in the shelves lining the neat wooden walls. They had been at sea a year already, ploughing on the tedious seven thousand mile journey. The *Greyhound* was a small ship. She had to choose her routes carefully, and sail when the winds were right. Her cargo of gold and ivory, dyer's wood and beeswax, took a long time to collect, although even when the hold was stacked full on the homeward journey, the cargo was light.

John was travelling as Captain Manesty's guest. He had his own cabin, and his place at the Captain's table. He had nothing to do, and all the time in the world to do it. At first he watched in delight as other people heaved and pulled and scrubbed and unloaded, but by the time they landed at Newfoundland, John was so bored with doing nothing that he joined the rest of the crew fishing for enormous cod off the icy coast. Their catch would be kept stored in the hold of the ship, to provide food for the home run.

The gales were already increasing, and he steadied himself against the shelves as the cabin lurched and the oil lamp spluttered and shook. In the calm that followed, he took out the first book that his hand touched.

It was called *The Imitation of Christ*, written by Thomas à Kempis. When John saw the title, he nearly put the book back in disgust. But he didn't. For some reason, he took it with him to the chair by his desk, and opened it. He read the first words he saw in the quavering light. "Life is short. Take care how you use it. Every work, word and thought ought to be ordered as if it was our last, as if we were about to die, and be asked to account for it."

John shut the book with a bang. He didn't want to read any more. Reading it made him wonder. It stirred a faint feeling of doubt in the back of his mind. It made him remember his mother. "As long as you do what is right," she had said, "God will love you." Her voice. Her words. The memory disturbed him. A voice was speaking to him out of the storm.

Impatiently he threw the book down, and went to bed.

* * *

He was woken before dawn by the sound of splintering wood. The cabin was filling with water, sweeping everything aside in its impatience. He struggled out of his hammock, grabbing his shirt before the water caught it and carried it away. As he struggled into it, there was an enormous crash, and then silence. More water swirled past him.

A terrified voice shrieked, "She's sinking!"

Pushing against the force of the water, John battled his way up on deck. There was pandemonium. The whole of the timber boarding one side of the upper deck had been broken and swept away. Teams of men worked the pumps furiously, while the rest of the crew baled water out of the ship with buckets. But they weren't equal to the great fifteen-foot waves that towered for a moment above them, and then crashed down through the masts on to the deck, filling the ship and bending and breaking everything in their way.

"Here!" Someone shoved a bucket into John's hands and he joined them trying to keep the ship afloat.

For the rest of the night, until the first light of dawn came through the black clouds, John worked with them, frantically throwing bucket after bucket of water into the swirling sea. The winds were icy, and the sea felt like cold steel, blinding the men as it lashed into their eyes. Then, as the light grew stronger, the wind began to die down a little, and for a moment, it was possible to speak.

John was on his way to relieve one of the men at the pumps. His hands were so numb and cold that he only knew they were still part of him because they hurt so much. The wind took his breath away.

"Give it a rest," the Captain suggested. "The

wind's slackening. Get some food—you need it."

"He's been at the pump all night," John nodded towards a young boy, pulling on the pump automatically, as if his body was working while his mind slept. "He can get some food and rest first. Then I'll go down."

"Right." The Captain nodded and John turned away.

"If this won't do," he added, almost as an afterthought, "then the Lord have mercy on us."

Captain Manesty stared after him in astonishment.

As John struggled to remain upright against the wind and the rain until he reached the pumps, his mind was in as much turmoil as the sea, threshing and churning all round him. "The Lord have mercy." Why had he said it? It had come naturally, as if it was part of him.

"Lord have mercy . . ." He repeated the words under his breath. But they frightened him. God might have mercy on the ship. He might save them from drowning. He might bring them safely home to dry land. "But why should he have mercy on me?"

He couldn't think properly. The water was still running so fast and so high that the ship seemed like a flat fish, just managing to swim along abreast of the water. The first wave that swept through the ship after John had taken over his side of the pump knocked him flat on his face. He pulled himself up and tied himself to the wooden structure holding the great levers in place. Then, in the effort of pushing and pulling against all the pressure of the water, he gave up trying to think.

Only later, as the rhythmic movement became part of him, and the constant battering of wind and rain and lashing waves numbed his mind, did he find his mother's words coming back again and again. "If you do what is right, God will love you. If you do what is right. If you do what is right. If you do what is right."

After nine hours, he stumbled below and fell into his hammock. He was so tired, he didn't much care whether he woke in Heaven or in Hell.

He woke again before he had been sleeping an hour. The shrill cries of "All hands on deck!" echoed through the ship, and he struggled to his feet, his arms and legs still aching and stiff from the strain of nine hours at the pumps.

"Here, Newton," Captain Manesty greeted him with relief. "Take the helm. Keep her in the wind —that's all you can do. And God be with you."

It was like a vast switchback, riding on the crest of the great high waves, and then plunging headlong down into the black hole that lay between them. And then the crashing and the darkness as the waves seemed to meet in an arch above. For a split second, the moon and the stars were obliterated. Then they appeared again, shining and still above the battered, broken ship.

John thought and thought. He tried to remember the phrases his mother had taught him from the Bible. But all he could remember was about sin and hell and eternal damnation. He tried to remember the excitement he had once felt when he read about Jesus. But his mind was too full of the wrong things he had said and done over the last few years. He looked up at the vast sky stretching above him. At the shining silver stars. At the great waves as they shattered the masts and splintered the decks.

And he was afraid.

The night became day. A cold grey March day, with bitter squalls whipping across the deck. There was no sun. There was just the constant squeaking of the pumps, and the frightened shriek and squeal of pigs, swept overboard and lost in the sea, as the force of the water broke into the hold.

Then the wind changed.

Where spars were still standing, sails were hoisted, and the wind began spinning the ship towards Ireland.

"The livestock's gone." Captain Manesty looked gravely at his crew. "The provisions were swept overboard last night. They smashed against the bows. There's codfish and pig food. If we're lucky, it'll last seven days."

There weren't many codfish. To ration them out, each fish was cut in half. Each half was one day's food for twelve men. It was very salty, and to try to drown the saltiness, they drank mug after mug of water from the vast butts stowed below decks, and untouched by the storm.

They had been sailing for five days, when there was a loud cry from the masts.

"Land! Land ahoy!"

A stampede from the cabins and the holds and the foc'sle, followed the cry, until the whole crew was rushing on deck to see if it was true.

They looked into the distance, and there was a high mountainous lump of land with one or two islands dotted off it. It was about twenty miles away, the shape and contours corresponding exactly with the north west points of Ireland.

An enormous cheer went up. Given a good wind and no more gales, they would be in the harbour safely within a day.

John led the joyful rush back below decks again. Captain Manesty, laughing and smiling for the first time in days, prised open the last cask of brandy, and handed round the precious ration. Eager hands, blistered and sore with the cold and the wet and the work, broke up the last pieces of coarse bread which had once been loaded on board to feed the pigs. Someone burst into song, and John felt a wave of warmth and relief tingeing the gloom that had blackened the last weeks.

He went up on deck alone. The islands were turning slowly from grey to palest pink. Then orange and deep red in the setting sun. In silence, the rest of the crew slowly joined John, and they watched the sun sink. It sank very gently and then died away, until it was no more than a purple smudge in the sky. It sank below the islands. And when it had gone, they remained: several heavy black clouds gathered threateningly on the horizon where the sea met the sky. They were an illusion.

The wind which had scudded along behind them, died away. The sea remained quite calm for a day and a night, with the *Greyhound* powerless to move forward or backward—and with only a few remaining salt cod shared out in thin portions between them. The next day a wind sprang up and began pushing the ship in the wrong direction.

It was such a nightmare that no one had time to notice the change that had come over John. For some reason, which he could not explain, he had stopped cursing and swearing. Suddenly he seemed to have forgotten the words.

For four days, the ship drifted. Then, at last, the breeze they longed for sprang up, and the sails were hoisted again. For a moment, it was touch and go whether the ropes were sound enough to pull the sails to the top of the few splintered masts that remained standing, and men began trying to climb the rigging, rotten and damp with strain. Then they were under way. As they sailed raggedly into harbour, the last pieces of fish were boiling on the galley stoves.

They had just dropped anchor, when the wind veered, and the gale which sprang up would have sunk the ship.

One by one, the men tottered unsteadily off the shattered ship and on to the crowded quay. Cheers went up. Hands shook theirs. They were surrounded by offers of food and drink and beds. John couldn't take in all that was happening. That night, as he lay down to sleep, between crisp clean sheets, after a supper of freshly baked bread and sizzling steak, his dreams were full of the sound of waves breaking on wood, and the smell of stale fish, steaming water, and cooking oil smoking on the stoves.

*   *   *

The next morning he was up early. The sea was still wild as he made his way up the cobbled street. Gulls were shrieking, wheeling backwards and forwards above his head. An old woman, spinning in a doorway, looked up as he passed. At the sight of his soiled clothes and sea-stained boots, a smile of welcome came over her face.

He reached the top of the hill. Then, hesitantly, he pushed open the door of the church, and the crying of the gulls and the crashing of the waves were lost in stillness. There was a cross on the holy table. For a long time, he stood and looked at it. Then, for the first time since he was ten years old, he knelt down.

He felt that Jesus was speaking to him. He knew that Jesus loved him and was asking him to give him his heart. He had hurt Jesus as much as any jeering soldier spitting in his face. He thought of the naked slaves on the *Pegasus*! In his own way he had helped to crucify Jesus. But Jesus had loved him all the time.

There, in the silence of the church, he spoke to Jesus. "I'm sorry," he whispered.

And for the first time in his life John Newton really meant it.

When he came out, the gulls were still calling. The sky was still heavy and threatening. The air was still wet and cold. He didn't know where he was going, or what he was going to do. He wasn't even sure that he knew what was right and what was wrong yet. But he knew that he had found God again, and for the moment, that was all that mattered.

One of the sailors met him before he reached the quay. He was running.

"We've emptied the hold," he gasped breathlessly. "They're starting repairs. You know the six full butts of water stowed away there?"

John nodded.

"They were marked full," he gulped, "but the storm had cracked them. Five were empty!"

8

FIRST MATE ON THE SLAVER

JOHN stood on the doorstep looking down at his new shoes with silver buckles, and the pale blue silk thread of his smart stockings. He had a ruffled shirt, a powdered wig and a blue cockaded three-cornered hat. His coat of rich blue silk had stiffening which made it flick out round the hem. He was dressed in the height of fashion. He was also a gentleman of some position. Since returning from Ireland he had been offered the command of a ship.

But he was petrified.

All the way from Liverpool to Chatham, he had rehearsed the words. Against the bumping and rattling of the stage coach, as it travelled across country from the North, he had tried writing them down. Time after time he had crossed them through and started all over again. The other travellers had watched him curiously. But John took no notice. Now he felt he was word perfect.

He just lacked the courage to ring the doorbell.

At last he grabbed the rope, and gave it such a strong pull that the enormous clanging of the bell nearly sent him running down the path again.

The door opened.

"John! Dear John! Come in at once out of the cold, and let us look at you."

Mary's mother drew him into the warm glow of the hall, where the dogs lay sleeping in front of a roaring fire.

"How he's grown, mother!" They all crowded round him.

"Yes. He looks older," said Mrs. Catlett, studying the new strength in John's face.

"And wiser," grunted Mary's father tersely. But he smiled at John, and led him into the dining room, where the roast meat was waiting on the side table to be cut off in juicy dripping hunks and piled on to John's plate.

"Tell us some stories, John," begged Jack, Mary's older brother, as they sat down to dinner. "Tell us where you've been. Tell us what you've done."

And as John couldn't pluck up the courage to ask outright where Mary was, he began to tell them stories. He told them about the storms and the islands in the sun, about the wild animals and the beautiful buildings and the exotic flowers, and he felt very wise and clever as they listened to him with bated breath and eyes wide with wonder.

"And then—Jack, you'll never believe this," he went on, "down the coast of Guinea, just beyond . . . just beyond . . ." he tailed off. They followed his eyes. The door had opened.

"Mary!" Mrs. Catlett welcomed her. "Where have you been? Look what a surprise we have for you!"

John stared as Mary came gracefully across to him and held out her hand for him to take.

"How nice to see you again, John," she smiled,

and he was so enchanted listening to her voice that he forgot to answer. After what seemed like an hour of silence, he spluttered stiffly, "Delighted to meet you again, ma'am", and was grateful to Jack for interrupting.

"John has been telling us the most marvellous stories, Mary," he said, pulling a chair to the table for her. "Tell us some more, John—they're so exciting. It's like going for a voyage round the world."

But all the wonderful words and colourful stories which had been rolling out of John so easily, had gone. His mind seemed quite blank and his tongue had turned to iron. He sat back, and let the others talk around him.

Once during the evening, Mr. Catlett turned to him. "You're back to Liverpool tomorrow, then, John?"

"I'm afraid so, sir." John found his tongue with difficulty.

"Sailing straight away?"

"I have to be there to see the loading finished," explained John, pleased to be able to indicate to Mary the responsibility that lay on his shoulders.

"But surely there's little enough cargo on the first passage?" asked Jack, anxious to widen his knowledge of the slave trade.

"Only enough goods and money for exchange," agreed John. "But there are the collars to be counted, and the irons, as well as provisions to be stowed."

Mary's gasp of horror was drowned in Jack's reply. "But John," she interrupted, before her brother had finished speaking, "why do you take irons on board?" She looked upset. John couldn't for the moment think why. "And what are collars?" she asked him.

"Slaves are ready to run or dive overboard in the middle of the ocean once you're out and away," he explained carelessly, refraining from adding that there was so much illness and so little food and such an extent of cruelty that many of them would happily have hung themselves from the masts. "Besides, we'd be in constant danger if they weren't chained. Collars are only for the troublesome ones." He laughed. "And there are enough of those."

Mary stared at him. "What a horrible job you have, John,' she said quietly. John look at her in amazement.

"It—it's very respectable, ma'am," he stammered. He had never had to justify his work before. "Slaves are little more than animals—they'd be no happier in their homes than they are where we take them. They're savages, Mary," he insisted earnestly. "They don't understand. They aren't people like you and me."

"Aren't they, John?" Mary pushed her plate away from her.

"No—no, of course not." The thought had never struck John before. "Of course not," he repeated. But if he had persuaded himself, he knew he hadn't persuaded Mary.

Later, when at last he managed to catch her alone for a moment, his tongue became steel again. All the fine phrases about love and marriage which he had worked out so carefully on the journey down were completely forgotten.

"It—it's so good to see you again, Mary," he managed to say, between clenched teeth.

"The pleasure is ours, to see *you*, John," she replied coolly, without a trace of nerves. John noticed that she said "ours", and not "mine", and his heart sank. For a moment, she was near to him, and he thought her grey eyes and curly dark hair even more beautiful than he had imagined them to be during the years he had been away.

What were the words? If only he could remember them. If only he could remember a single phrase. A single word. They had looked so good and bold written down in black and white, but now he knew that even if he could remember them, he would never dare say them.

"Mary," he began hesitantly.

"Yes," she encouraged him gently.

"Mary, if I write to you," he paused. He paused for so long that Mary let out a sigh of impatience and began to turn away.

"Mary, if I write to you, will you promise to read the letter?" he said in a rush.

"I suppose it would be rude not to, if the letter was addressed to me," she retorted icily. "Of course I would."

Tossing her head in exasperation, she turned and went out of the room, and John was sure from the coldness of her voice that he had lost all chance of ever making her love him enough to marry him. He had no idea that outside the door, Mary didn't know whether to laugh or cry, she was so disappointed.

He wrote the letter on the coach back up North again. "Bestow a thought on me," he begged her. "Don't too hastily make it impossible for me to show all the world that I am your most faithful and ardent admirer and servant."

The letter which came back to him, just as he was to sail from the South Dock for Madeira, was very correct. "I wish you God speed on your voyage, and a safe homecoming," she wrote. "At present," the words danced as John read them, "at present, I have no intention or desire to marry while you are away".

That morning, as they set sail under grey skies from the dirty Liverpool docks, the wet decks of the ship *Brownlow* seemed to John to be paved with gold. He had asked for one journey as First Mate, before taking over the responsibility of captaining a slave ship. He had his own cabin. He had good pay. He had Mary to come home to when the long run was over. He gave the order for one of the crew to begin sorting the iron collars and manacles and chains ready for the first cargo of slaves, and then he went below decks to dine on oysters and port at the Captain's table.

* * *

Many months later he stood on deck in the first hazy sunlight, and watched as a small, familiar lump of land appeared, at first just faintly out-lined, and then clearer and clearer as the ship sailed in and dropped anchor beyond the jagged rocks showing below the surface of the calm green water.

"Newton!"

"Ay, ay, sir."

"We usually pick up a big consignment here. Who's taking the boat ashore?"

"I am, sir."

"Right. Be back before sundown, then we can be off while the winds are right." Captain Hardy turned to search among his papers. "I'll just find the name of the trader on this part of the coast."

"It's all right." John was looking across at the islands, straining his eyes in the mist to try to see more clearly. "I know his name. It's Clow."

"Hard round, and in to starboard!" John sat in the stern of the boat, directing his crew. "Tie her up by the landing beyond the cove."

The long white house looked the same. Hens rummaged in the huts outside. The narrow, open-decked boat was tied up the other side of the rough, makeshift landing as it always had been. It still had rings where Clow had secured the chain. Only one thing was different. Around the island, the limes had grown. They were no longer thin, weak saplings. They were young strong green trees, covering the island, weighed down with green and yellow fruit.

As John stepped ashore, a big man came out of the house and waved and shouted to them.

"I'm coming down!"

John came to meet him.

"Good day, Mr. Clow. Compliments of Captain Hardy of the *Brownlow*, trading from Liverpool, sir."

John swept off his hat politely. But he couldn't bring himself to do the customary bow.

Amos Clow's mouth dropped open. The red in his cheeks spread through his face and round the back of his neck. He coughed to hide his embarrassment.

"Newton! Bless my soul, Newton. It's—it's," he coughed and spluttered again. "It's—well, it's good to see you. Yes," he began to recover himself. "Yes, that's the word—good. It's good to see you. We thought—I thought—I mean, we thought you were . . ." He mopped his forehead with a large, not very clean silk handkerchief. "I mean, we always thought you'd make a success of life," he righted himself hurriedly. "What can I do for you? Come up to the house." He bustled on ahead of John. "You must have a meal while they load. I'll give the orders and make arrangements, and then I'll give you the best meal you've had since you left England."

He hurried on, puffing and panting, sending servants scampering off right and left, to open the best wine and kill the best turkey and pick the best fruit.

As they climbed the hill to the house, John struck a lime down from a tree.

"You have a good crop of limes, Mr. Clow," he remarked, smiling at him. "Try one."

Clow strode on, ignoring the interruption.

"They were well planted in good straight rows, I see," persisted John.

The sun was hot on the verandah. Far away, John could hear the shouts of his men as they herded the slaves on to the boat. Clow hurried off to see that dinner was under way, and John lay back in the long, low wicker chair. He could see the brilliant red and purple of flowers twisting up the verandah and curling across the roof. The perfume from them was sweet and heavy. He lay back again and closed his eyes.

He heard a scuffling by the door, but it was too warm and comfortable to pay any attention. If it was Clow coming back, he'd know soon enough. But it wasn't Clow. Although his eyes were still closed, John was sure he was being watched.

"It's Newton!"

He knew the voice. For a moment he couldn't place it. Then, as he opened his eyes, he heard another familiar voice whispering in astonishment, "Newton! With shoes on! And stockings too!" He met the wide-eyed gaze of the two slaves who had brought him their own rice and water rations when he had been sick with fever. As soon as they realized he had seen them, they ran away to the plantations as fast as their feet would carry them.

But all that day, John couldn't forget their words, or the look in their eyes. He dined with Amos Clow off the same gilt and gold plates, served by many of the same servants, their eyes politely turned away. Then he took his boat back to the *Brownlow*. But instead of giving him the gloating pleasure he had expected, the visit had made him feel uneasy.

He watched the slaves rounded up on deck, and then driven down to their quarters below by sailors with long whips in their hands. Later, when he went to make his inspection, he stood and watched them for a moment, sandwiched in tiny spaces like books in a bookcase, with barely room to turn, manacled together by their wrists, their faces full of bewilderment. They couldn't understand where they were being taken or what was going to happen to them, and they sobbed and cried together, calling out for help.

For the first time, John realized that if his skin had been black instead of white, he might well have been among the slaves Clow sold to the Guinea ships on their way to America. Because without shoes and without stockings, only the colour of his skin was different.

"When I'm a captain," he swore to himself solemnly, "I shall try to be kind to the slaves as well as to my crew."

9

IN COMMAND OF THE SHIP

"YOU see those stars?" John pointed into the clear night sky, where seven white stars shone brightly above them. "They call that the Little Bear."

Mary leaned nearer to him where they sat together on the grassy bank, and looked where he pointed.

"The Little Bear spends his life swinging by his tail from the Pole Star—that big, brilliant star right above us!"

Mary laughed with delight. And John's memory travelled miles, as he sat with his arm round her.

"There's something very safe about the Pole Star," he said, thoughtfully. "Wherever you are, across half the world, it's there. It's so bright and strong. I remember . . ." He thought of the storms and the miserable nights digging up roots with his hands and eating them raw, of the dangers and adventures. "I remember thinking that whatever happened, that bright star would still be there, to show me the way."

Mary had been quiet and serious all day. Now she smiled. "I'm glad you showed me, John," she said. "Now, when you leave me tomorrow, I can see that star at night, and every night afterwards until you come home, and know that you may be looking at it too. And if you are, it will be shining on us both."

John helped her up. She had been sitting on his new coat—the smart, braided and tucked coat of a captain. He brushed it down before he put it on again. Then they walked home, hand in hand.

They had been married five months. The next day, John boarded the stage waggon for Liverpool to begin a three-year voyage, commanding his own slave ship.

*   *   *

Before the ship sailed, John had an argument. Captain Manesty had come to see the *Duke of Argyle* leave Liverpool with John in command. He ran his experienced eye over the lists of provisions and goods being loaded.

His long finger moved down the paper. "Sixty iron collars . . ." His finger stopped. He frowned.

"You'll need more than sixty collars, if you take my advice, Captain Newton," he said.

But John had no intention of taking his advice. He hated the sight of the big iron rings, but he took them because he knew his crew might mutiny if he didn't.

"I don't think so." He searched for an argument that would carry weight. "They make marks on the men's necks, and bring the prices down. I don't think we'll need many."

Captain Manesty shrugged his shoulders and

went off shaking his head. He said no more. John was his own boss now. He would have to learn.

The captains commanding the other slave ships hovering in and out along the Guinea Coast, had never met anyone like John before.

In the evenings, they drank together, smoking and talking, gathered together in one of their cabins.

"Had a bad night!" growled one, downing his mug of rum. He had been kept awake by the crying of a baby belonging to a woman slave.

"I told her to silence it," he said, swaggering across the cabin. "But it went on crying. So I silenced it myself. I tore it away from her and threw it overboard."

John shuddered. He knew the man wasn't boasting. He meant what he said.

The long voyage dragged on. Mary and John wrote to each other and the letters piled up for John at each port. At the bottom of the ship, the cramped quarters were slowly filling. More and more slaves were brought on board. John had to use all his wits to avoid being cheated, and, almost without realizing what was happening, he found himself doing all the things he had hated so much in other captains of slave ships.

He studied the frightened prisoners as they were pushed and chivvied off the little boats which had brought them from the shore. He noted their age, their strength, their health and their handsomeness. If they were too old, he sent them back. If they were too small or too weak, he refused them. When he saw a man or a woman or a child that he knew would fetch a good price, he argued and shouted until he had made the best possible bargain. Then when the terrible middle passage began, shipping the frightened cargo from Africa to the West Indies and America, he found out the truth of Captain Manesty's words.

Illness began to spread through the slaves and to some of the crew. Men threatened to mutiny unless the slaves were kept quieter. Two of the slaves managed to slip their chains and were discovered rifling the rum casks. Two more tried to jump overboard. Reluctantly John ordered steel bits to be put between the teeth of the slaves who were so miserable and frightened, or so defiant that they refused to eat. He had the mutineers flogged and the others put in iron collars like yoked oxen.

"It has to be done," he told himself time and again. "How else can the trade be carried on? I have a duty to my job. For their own good, I must do it as well as I can."

Slavery was accepted without question as part of life. It was as easy then as it is now to take things for granted. To believe they are natural because they have become part of the picture, like wars and hunger and disease. John had a job to do. He wanted to do it as kindly and honestly as he could. But it never occurred to him to ask himself whether what he was doing was right.

Great cheers went up when at last the West Indies came in sight. Even the slaves, chained up on deck, began to cheer too. They didn't know that life on the plantations would be so hard that they would long to be back chained on board ship again. They didn't know that the longest a slave lived on the plantations was nine years. They cheered and cheered. And John, watching them, felt suddenly sorry.

"Wear them out quick, that's my motto," explained one man, as he bought ten strong boys from John for a very good price.

"Wouldn't kindness encourage better service?" suggested John. But he knew he might as well have said nothing.

The man's mouth fell open. "Kindness!" He roared with laughter. "They don't understand the meaning of the word. A kick and a sound beating works wonders. Wear them out quickly while there's plenty in them and then buy a new load. That way you get the most out of them."

John looked at the ten boys, their eyes full of fear as they were led off to their new life. He felt as if he had killed them.

As he sat in his cabin, he remembered Jesus on the cross. Jesus died for these slave boys as well as for him, John Newton. He could hear sobbing and moaning in the slaves' quarters, and he was the cause of their misery and suffering. As he took up his pen to write to Mary, John felt that his days as a slave ship captain were coming to an end. He had begun to question his work.

But when he came home, he was congratulated because fewer slaves had died on his run than on any voyage before. He was pleased with the praise, but he knew Mary hated the work that he did. Yet, he argued with himself, it was secure. It brought him enough money to buy her a new gown and a new hat when he came home; enough for them to visit the theatre and entertain their friends. He made two journeys. Long journeys lasting for years, to the Guinea Coast, to the Americas, and home, and each time he longed to see Mary's face waiting in Liverpool to welcome him when the ship docked at last.

He didn't know, when she threw her arms round him and begged him not to go away again so soon, that the second voyage was the last long one he would make.

A few weeks after the ship berthed, they were sitting quietly at home together. It was evening, and the flames from the fire flickered across the room. It was all very peaceful and pleasant.

"Polly?"

Mary smiled as John used his pet name for her. She came across and sat down on the floor beside him. He put his arm round her. "Do you know, Polly," he went on, "I'm happier than I ever dreamed of being."

She smiled up at him. But as he opened his mouth to tell her how much he loved her, as he told her time and again, she felt his arm slacken on her shoulder. The next moment, he had fallen on the floor.

John was only 30 years old. The stroke he had was only a mild one, and by the next day, he seemed almost well again. But it meant that he would never command his own ship on a long voyage again.

*   *   *

It was just seven o'clock in the morning. John sat on a stile and watched the world waking up.

Above him, so high he could hardly see it, a lark sang. From the river, the coarse croak of a black moorhen bobbing busily backwards and forwards made its own funny kind of music. The constant clear babbling of a brook passing almost under his feet added its own part to the orchestra.

And there were the colours. John gazed about him in delight. The sky, rapidly turning from pale to deep bright blue as the sun gained strength. The grass, brilliant green, bordering the yellow corn. Scarlet poppies, and the green and brown and gold and crimson of a pheasant strutting through the bracken.

In the stillness which seemed so full of music and colour and beauty, John climbed from the stile and knelt down where he was. The leaves made marks on his velvet breeches, but he didn't care. He was in a temple far more beautiful than any of the solid stone churches, because God had made it with his own hands.

There he gave himself to God. In full surrender John Newton handed his life to God for service to Jesus Christ. Kneeling by the stile, he prayed that God would use him as a preacher of the Gospel. "Take all I have, Lord," he said. "All I am and all I can be."

When he strode home, almost running in his eagerness to tell Mary his decision, the world seemed alive with all the lovely things he had never noticed before.

"What would you say, Polly," he asked her eagerly, almost before he was in the door, "what would you say if I was to give up everything and become a minister in the Church of England?"

10

PREACHER AND PROPHET

"Let the world deride or pity,
I will glory in Thy name!"

John could write bold, exciting hymns. It was a
different matter when he came to preach his
first sermon.

He could hear it in his mind.

"I shan't need notes," he insisted obstinately to
Mary before leaving home. "I know what I
believe. That's enough."

He strode to the pulpit of the Leeds church and
began climbing the spiral staircase. When he
reached the top, he put down his Bible and looked
round. Below him, a sea of up-turned faces
waited expectantly. John cleared his throat. And
the people sat down.

John cleared his throat again

Suddenly he felt embarrassed. His face must
look so rough and weather-beaten from the years
he had spent at sea. And his voice! How many
times Mary had begged him to keep his voice
down.

"You're not at sea now, John!" she laughed, as
he barked his words out awkwardly. He looked
again at the faces below him. If he didn't bark at
them, he'd probably whisper, and they would
hear nothing.

John's cheeks grew redder, and the silence grew longer.

He had forgotten every word of his sermon.

Slowly, very slowly, he turned round and walked the long, long way down the stairs and out of the church.

"I'm never going to preach again," he told Mary, almost in tears.

"Oh, yes," she said soothingly. "Oh, yes, you will."

But he didn't try to preach again for two years. Somehow it didn't seem right to preach to people who had been going to church for years, when John himself had only so recently learned to love God instead of hating Him.

Then at last he agreed to try again. Night after night he sat up late writing and re-writing, until the candle flickered and spluttered and burned itself out. And when at last the day came, John took his long, detailed notes into the pulpit with him, and holding them near to his nose, because he was becoming short-sighted, he muttered through word for word from beginning to end, without raising his voice or lifting his eyes from the papers in front of him in case he forgot his words.

When the sermon ended, one or two people were fast asleep!

It wasn't until six years later, when he had become curate of Olney in Buckinghamshire that John found that if you loved God enough, He really did put thoughts into your heart and words into your mouth. Every Sunday as he walked across the green meadows towards the little church, John knew that nearly two thousand people would be coming for miles to squash their way into the pews to hear what he had to say. Why they came, he couldn't imagine. But he smiled with the joy and excitement of it all.

One of John's greatest friends at Olney was a poet called William Cowper. He came regularly on a Sunday to hear John preach, and then to the massive lunches Mary prepared for all the parishioners who had travelled more than six miles to the church.

Sometimes when John said grace for them, he used the words of his own little hymn:

"May the grace of Christ our Saviour
And the Father's boundless love,
With the Holy Spirit's favour,
Rest upon us from above.

Thus may we abide in union
With each other and the Lord,
And possess in sweet communion,
Joys which earth cannot afford."

And afterwards, he and William Cowper used to wander out into the fields until they came to the stile by the stream, where they would sit talking together, watching the clouds sailing through the sky and the birds chattering in the trees.

Cowper seemed to be a happy man, yet sometimes John would see a shadow come across his face, and he would be suddenly very serious.

Gradually John began to realize that really he was a very sad person. He was sad because God seemed so very far away that he didn't seem to be a friend at all.

"Oh for a closer walk with God," Cowper wrote—because, like John, he too composed hymns. "A calm and heavenly frame. A light to shine upon the road that leads me to the Lamb."

"I wish there was something I could do to make William smile," John used to say to Mary, when they were at home together in the evenings.

"Let's invite him here to stay with us," said Mary suddenly. "And then he could see how happy we are, and how close to God you are, and he might learn to know Jesus as a friend, like you do!"

And so they did, and John enjoyed having his friend with him. It was fun to have someone to come walking—a man who could step out and cover the miles and not be afraid of the cows standing solidly chewing and following you around with their eyes. Bit by bit, John told Cowper about his adventures at sea. And Cowper never seemed to tire of hearing. He even found the words John had said creeping into the verses he wrote:

"God moves in a mysterious way," began one of his hymns,

"His wonders to perform;
He plants his footsteps in the sea,
And rides upon the storm."

One day, he read his hymns to John, and John listened. And as he listened, his excitement grew.

"I've an idea!" He could hardly wait until his friend finished reading the last line. "I've an idea— such a very good idea!"

William Cowper stopped and listened.

"We'll publish a book of hymns! You and me—we'll write verses to explain the pieces we love best from the Bible. And we'll have them print it and use it in the churches: 'Olney Hymns, by Mr. Cowper and Mr. Newton'!"

For the first time in months, a slow smile shone for a moment in Cowper's eyes. It could almost have been a smile of enthusiasm.

"All right." He put out his hand to John and their eyes met. "All right. I think I'd like that very much."

And that night, as they sat round the open fire, with logs piled high in the grate, John felt so happy and close to God that he said quietly the little blessing he had composed:

> "Now may He who from the dead
> Brought the Shepherd of the sheep,
> Jesus Christ, our king and head,
> All our souls in safety keep."

When he finished, he saw Cowper's lips form the word "Amen", and he felt that perhaps the Rev. John Newton might be able to be of some use to God after all.

11

THE END OF SLAVE TRADING

IT was seven o'clock on a cold winter morning, many years later when a rich young man set out from his apartments in the Strand, a mile or two away from the Rectory of St. Mary Woolnoth in London. The young man was well known. So well known that people turned and stared as he passed. Some whispered and pointed, but he took no notice. He was very preoccupied. Slowly he walked along Fleet Street towards Ludgate Hill and the City of London.

As he turned left off Cannon Street, towards the Bank of England, an elderly gentleman recognized him.

"Mr. Wilberforce!"

The old man stood before him and forced him to stop. He was annoyed. Since the Gallery of the House of Commons had been opened to the public, many people recognized him in the street, but he was too busy with his own thoughts to want to be bothered with strangers.

"I must congratulate you—a splendid speech you made in the House last night. You and Mr. Pitt will make the country great again, mark my words!"

William Wilberforce bowed politely, murmured nothing in particular and skirted around his admirer. Then he continued pacing on his way, head down, brows furrowed, deep in thought. No one else dared to approach him.

When he arrived at the door of the Rev. John Newton who had become Rector of St. Mary's, the church in Lombard Street near the busy wool exchange where the merchants bought and sold all day, he hesitated.

"What shall I say to him?" He shook his head. In the House of Commons it was easy to speak. At parties and hunting at weekends, it was easier still. But now—he shook his head again. At last, he strode up the steps and rang the bell.

The grey-haired man who met him in a study lined deep with books, had a strong, square face, and shrewd eyes. The young M.P. sat down with a sigh of relief. Perhaps it wasn't going to be so hard after all.

"You wrote to me," began John coaxingly. "What's the trouble?"

"I need help," said the young man, simply, the rich ruffles of his shirt fluttering elegantly from graceful fingers.

"I have money. I can gamble at any one of five of the most exclusive clubs in London and lose a hundred pounds a night, and still I'm rich. I have friends. They ask me constantly to join their shooting parties and to laugh and drink and play the fool at their masquerades. They take pleasure in adding my name to their lists of acquaintances. Now that they have opened the Gallery in the House, not only my name is known all over the country, but my face all over London. The Prime

Minister invites me to breakfast with him every week. I am cheered when I make a speech. "I am," he smiled ruefully, "very popular."

John smiled too. "But you're not happy?" he asked.

"No. There is something missing. I have read your sermons. I have heard you preach. The things you talk about mean more to me than any of the others. But what can I do? If I attach myself to a church, I shall be eaten up by the minister and congregation. If I preach at the Prime Minister, he tells me I am going mad, and advises me to stick to politics. The life I've been leading is wrong, but what is right? You are the only person I know who can help me."

He sat back, and mopped his brow with a yellow silk handkerchief. A very rich and a very popular young man, he was unused to confessing his sins.

John Newton sat for a moment, looking out of his study window across the busy city streets. He was remembering a night long ago. The cracking of broken masts. The noise of ripping canvas and splintering boards. The howling of the wind. And in the middle of it all, sudden peace of mind.

Young Wilberforce leaned forward impatiently.

"I'll do anything," he offered eagerly. "Give up my friends. Disown my family. Give up my career in Parliament and become a monk . . ."

Newton turned back from the window. He studied the young man for a moment.

"I don't think that you should give up anything," he said quietly. "Neither your friends, nor your position, nor your convictions. Hold on to them all. There is room in Parliament for men like you. Stay there—and see where God will take you. I was like you," John continued. "I was lost, and disgusted with myself. I wanted adventure and rebellion. I had done wrong, and I wanted to know what was right. And yet I went on for nearly ten years doing something which I now know was brutal and inhuman. But the lessons I learned from those years, I shall never forget." He shuddered as his hand touched the pages of the diary he was writing.

"I hope that what I learned will one day be used to end our trading in slaves. Then my life will be complete. You, Mr. Wilberforce, could lead the campaign to end slave trading. I have been a captain of a slave ship and I know the brutal in-humanity of this vile trade. The conscience of Britain needs rousing and only someone like you in the House of Commons can do it. You can speak to the soul of the British people as a Christian man. You, Mr. Wilberforce, have been called by God as his messenger. You can bring slave trading to an end. As a servant of the Lord Jesus, I hope you will lead the great campaign."

William Wilberforce was very thoughtful as he rose from his knees and made his way back from the City to his home in the West End.

*   *   *

It was the 25th of March, 1807.

William Wilberforce ran up Lombard Street. Mud splashed on to his breeches from the horses and the waggons hurrying by, but he didn't care.

He had news. Wonderful news. And he wanted John Newton to be the first to hear it.

The cheers that had greeted him from all over the House of Commons were still ringing in his ears. There had been opposition. Bitter opposition. But the facts about the slave trade, many of them authenticated by passages from Newton's diary, had helped him to carry the Bill through Parliament.

Edging through the stalls and barrows crowding the narrow city streets, he arrived at the Rectory at last. Wilberforce sprang up the steps in a single bound, and impatiently—because he was always impatient—he jangled the bell.

He knew that something was wrong as soon as the maid opened the door.

"I wanted Mr. Newton to be the first to hear," he explained. "I wanted to tell him myself. I wanted him to know that the Bill abolishing the slave trade was given the Royal Assent today. But . . ." he trailed off.

The maid smiled at his eagerness.

"Mr. Newton heard, sir," she told him gently. "They told him the news. It came through just before he lost consciousness."

Wilberforce turned. All the excitement and rush and hurry had suddenly gone out of the day. But John Newton had heard the news. And that was all that mattered.

The maid smiled at him again. "It made him very happy, sir," she added.

John Newton was 82 years old, and his work was done. As he always said, God planned things very well.